SPACE TECHNOLOGY

BY JANIE HAVEMEYER

childsworld.com

ABOUT THE AUTHOR

Janie Havemeyer is an author of many books for young readers. She has a master's degree in education and has taught in schools. Havemeyer lives in San Francisco, California. She watched the Apollo 11 Moon landing live on her television set when she was ten years old.

The Child's World
childsworld.com

Published by The Child's World®
800-599-READ • www.childsworld.com

Photography Credits
Photographs ©: NASA, cover, 1, 5, 9, 10, 14, 17, 18; Detlev van Ravenswaay/Science Source, 6; Neil A. Armstrong/NASA, 12; A. Simon, M.H. Wong, and the OPAL team/STScI/ESA/NASA, 19; JPL-Caltech/MSSS/NASA, 20; JPL-Caltech/NASA, 22; USAF 30th Space Wing/Anthony Men/NASA, 24; Kim Shiflett/NASA, 27; Bill Ingalls/NASA, 28

ISBN Information
9781503869868 (Reinforced Library Binding)
9781503881334 (Portable Document Format)
9781503882645 (Online Multi-user eBook)
9781503883956 (Electronic Publication)

LCCN 2022951224

Printed in the United States of America

BRINGING THE WORLD TO YOUNG READERS 1968

CONTENTS

FAST FACTS

- *Sputnik 1* was launched in 1957. It was the first time anyone had sent a **satellite** to space.
- An R-7 rocket launched *Sputnik 1* into **orbit**. This rocket was first designed to carry weapons.
- In 1969, the first person walked on the Moon. This space walk was part of the Apollo 11 mission.
- The A7L space suit was made for the Apollo 11 mission. It kept astronauts alive while they weren't connected to their spacecraft.
- The Hubble Space Telescope was sent to space in 1990. But it had a flaw in one of its mirrors. After astronauts repaired it in 1993, it took clear pictures of deep space.
- In 2012, *Curiosity* became the biggest **rover** to explore Mars. Scientists invented new technology so it could safely land there.
- The Falcon 9 is a reusable rocket. It was invented by SpaceX. In 2015, the Falcon 9 successfully landed back on Earth for the first time.

Developments in space technology have allowed humans to explore the universe and understand Earth's place in it. ►

CHAPTER ONE

SPUTNIK 1

Eight-year-old Bonnie Dunbar looked up at the sky. It was night on her family's farm in Washington State. She saw the Moon and stars in the dark sky. But on that October night in 1957, Bonnie knew there was something else up there. Somewhere far above her, a small satellite travelled through space. Bonnie looked hard, but she couldn't spot it.

Far away, in a country called the Soviet Union, scientists had been hard at work. On October 4, they launched the first **artificial** satellite into space. It was called *Sputnik 1*. It flew inside a powerful rocket. The satellite was about the size of a beach ball. It orbited Earth once every 96 minutes. *Sputnik 1* gathered information about the **atmosphere** and sent the data back to Earth.

◄ ***Sputnik 1*** **had four long antennae to send signals back to Earth.**

It was a complicated task to send something into space. One challenge was escaping Earth's gravity. Gravity is the force that keeps objects on the ground. A rocket needs to be very powerful to fight gravity and reach space. Another challenge was designing a rocket that would keep spacecraft safe on their way into orbit. But the Soviet Union had done it.

The US government was concerned. The Soviet Union was a powerful rival of the United States at that time. Some people wished that the United States had sent a satellite to space first. Other people worried that the rocket used to launch *Sputnik 1* could carry weapons.

The rocket was called the R-7. Sergei Korolev led the team that designed the R-7. The rocket was made to carry a **nuclear warhead** all the way to the United States. But the Soviet Union realized that the rocket could do more. It could also send a peaceful satellite into space.

On October 4, 1957, the R-7 blasted off with *Sputnik 1* in the tip of the rocket. When the R-7 reached space, it released *Sputnik 1* into orbit. The mission was accomplished.

Americans poured out of their homes, trying to catch a glimpse of *Sputnik 1* as it orbited Earth. Two radio transmitters on the satellite sent beeping signals down to Earth. Americans could tune in and hear the steady beeps on their own radios.

▲ **During her time as a NASA astronaut, Bonnie Dunbar flew five missions to space.**

After *Sputnik 1*, the US government pledged to catch up to the Soviet Union in space exploration. This was the start of what would become known as the Space Race. A few months later, the United States launched its own satellite, *Explorer 1*. Throughout the Space Race, the United States and the Soviet Union would each try to create more advanced technology for space exploration. Eventually, new kinds of rockets would launch humans into space.

One of these humans was Bonnie Dunbar. Hearing about *Sputnik 1* as a child had inspired her to explore space herself. She became an astronaut in 1981, 24 years after she searched the skies for *Sputnik 1*.

CHAPTER TWO

THE A7L SPACE SUIT

On July 20, 1969, American astronaut Neil Armstrong opened the hatch of a spacecraft. He was the commander of the Apollo 11 space mission. Their team had safely landed the spacecraft on the moon. Buzz Aldrin, one of Armstrong's partners, waited to follow him outside.

Armstrong backed out of the hatch. He put both feet on the top rung of the ladder. He was dressed in the newest space suit. It had been invented for the Apollo program. It was called the A7L. It was more advanced than earlier space suits. In the old suits, astronauts breathed oxygen through hoses attached to their spacecraft. They needed to stay close to their spacecraft to get air. But in the A7L space suits, Armstrong and Aldrin could wander away from their spacecraft.

◄ **Buzz Aldrin was the second person to walk on the moon.**

▲ **On the Moon, the Sun's energy can be harmful. The A7L helmet had a special coating to protect astronauts. The coating helped astronauts see clearly, too.**

When the astronauts were near their spacecraft, they still breathed through hoses. But sometimes they had to walk farther away. Their space suits had their own life-support systems. These systems kept the astronauts alive and safe while away from their ship.

Each astronaut's space suit had a backpack that held the life-support equipment. It had electricity, a fan, and oxygen for breathing. It also got rid of the carbon dioxide that the astronauts breathed out. It contained a water tank for drinking.

The water also cooled the astronauts down. The backpack had a radio to communicate with Earth and the other astronauts.

It had taken hundreds of skilled people to design and make the A7L. It had 21 layers of fabric. Each layer had a purpose. Some layers helped keep astronauts the right temperature. The surface of the moon can get as hot as 250 degrees Fahrenheit (121°C) in sunlight. It can get as cold as negative 280 degrees Fahrenheit (-173°C) in the shade. Other layers **pressurized** the suit. They protected astronauts from dangerous types of energy in space, too. The suit weighed about 180 pounds (82 kg) on Earth but only 30 pounds (14 kg) on the Moon. The Moon has one-sixth the gravity of Earth. That means things weigh six times less on the Moon than they do on Earth.

Armstrong wore his space suit as he placed one foot on the gray, powdery surface of the moon. "That's one small step for man, one giant leap for mankind," he said. Armstrong had become the first person to set foot on the moon.

Astronauts in the future may need to live in space longer. Space suit technology is advancing to meet mission needs. Suits have become more formfitting. They use new fabrics and stronger materials. Suits are easier to get on and off. They are also being designed for comfort. Astronauts will be able to walk and move more freely in future space suits.

CHAPTER THREE

THE HUBBLE SPACE TELESCOPE

The space shuttle *Endeavour* pierced the morning sky on December 2, 1993. *Endeavour* was one of five space shuttles. These reusable spacecraft carried astronauts into orbit between 1981 and 2011. On this flight, *Endeavour* was on a mission to repair the Hubble Space Telescope.

Hubble was the first telescope of its kind launched into space. Earth's atmosphere and clouds make it hard for telescopes on Earth to get clear pictures of space. But Hubble is in orbit 350 miles (563 km) above Earth's surface. This is high enough for Hubble to take very clear pictures of deep space. It sends these pictures back to scientists on Earth. Hubble's pictures have helped scientists make many discoveries. They revealed two moons of Pluto. They helped confirm that the universe is over 13 billion years old.

◄ **It takes the Hubble Space Telescope about an hour and a half to orbit Earth.**

But after Hubble launched in 1990, its pictures came back blurry. The telescope uses two curved mirrors to reflect light. Scientific instruments use this light to create images. Once Hubble was in space, scientists realized that its main mirror was the wrong shape.

The mirror's shape was wrong by a tiny fraction of an inch. But this was enough to ruin the pictures. Scientists planned a mission to fix the telescope. Hubble had been designed to be repaired in space. It could stay up-to-date with technology because astronauts could replace old parts of the telescope with newer ones. The future of Hubble was riding on the success of *Endeavour*'s mission.

Two days after leaving Earth, *Endeavour* reached Hubble. Astronaut Claude Nicollier extended the shuttle's 50-foot (15 m) robotic arm. The arm grabbed a hook on the telescope and pulled Hubble into the shuttle's cargo bay. Cheers broke out in mission control back on Earth.

Seven astronauts prepared to repair Hubble. Four of them would perform multiple space walks over five days. Astronauts Kathryn Thornton and Thomas Akers would correct Hubble's blurry vision.

Kathryn Thornton and the other astronauts prepared for their mission by training in a pool. Underwater, they floated like they would in space. ►

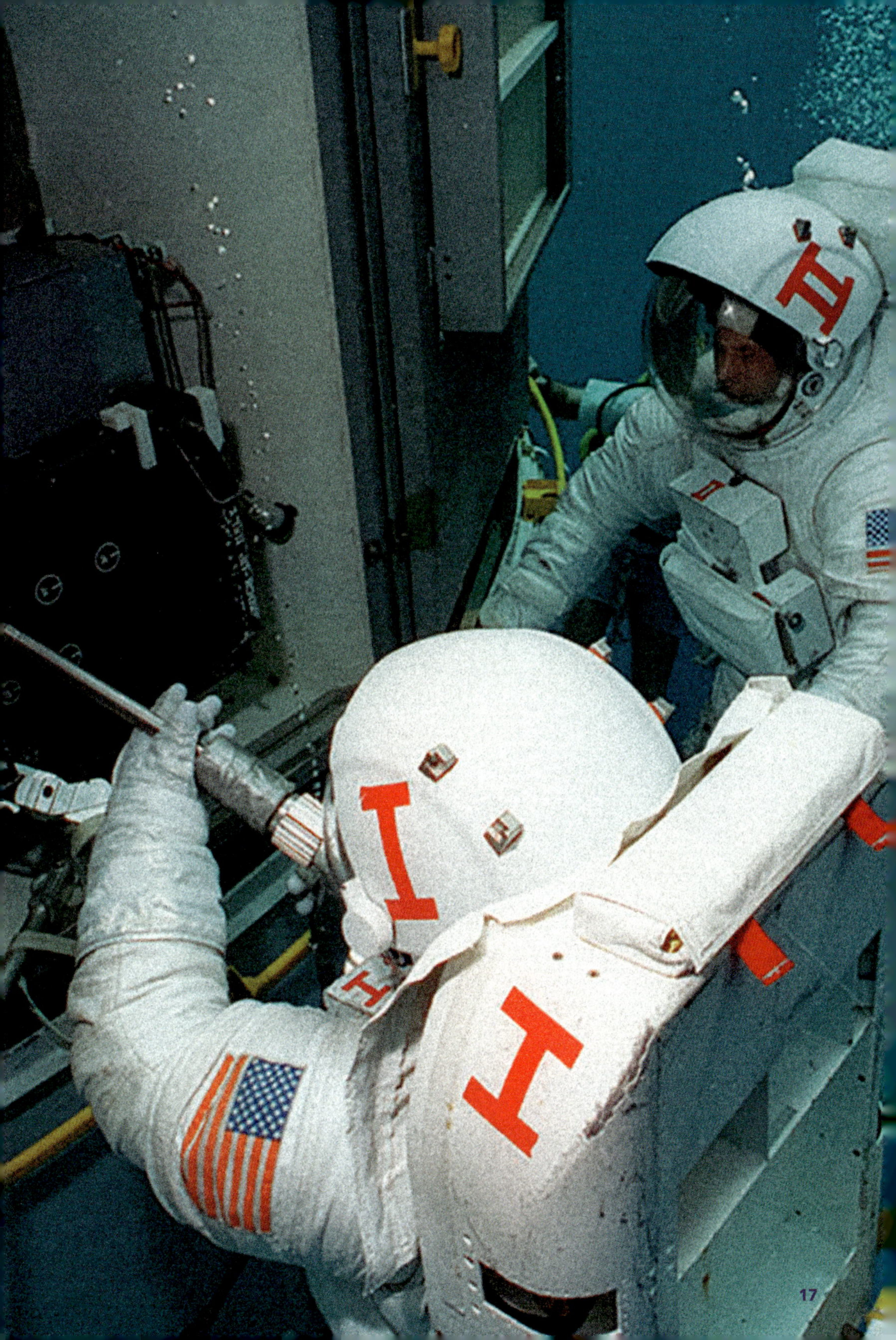

▲ Kathryn Thornton and Thomas Akers placed COSTAR on the telescope during the fourth spacewalk of their mission.

Thornton fitted her space boots into foot restraints. These would make sure she didn't float away. *Endeavour*'s robotic arm guided her into position. She gripped a device called COSTAR in both hands. COSTAR was around the size of a refrigerator. It weighed 1,520 pounds (690 kg) on Earth. But in orbit it was weightless. COSTAR was a new camera. It had been designed to fix Hubble's vision. Its mirrors were shaped to correct the main mirror's flaw. It was nicknamed Hubble's glasses.

Hubble's next photograph arrived five days after *Endeavour* returned to Earth. The picture of a star was sharp and clear.

▲ **The Hubble Space Telescope can take detailed images of other planets. For example, it shows how a storm on Jupiter called the Great Red Spot changes shape and color.**

Hubble's vision was perfect. The space telescope started a new age of **astronomy**. The telescope answered many questions about planets, stars, and galaxies.

Four more repair missions followed this one. But the space shuttle program ended in 2011. After that, Hubble was no longer maintained. A new telescope was launched into orbit in 2021. It is called the James Webb Space Telescope. It can look deeper into space and capture more information than Hubble could.

CHAPTER FOUR

CURIOSITY'S SKY CRANE

Scientists crowded together in NASA's Jet Propulsion Laboratory (JPL) on August 5, 2012. The *Curiosity* rover was about to land on Mars. The team listened as a scientist reported each step of *Curiosity*'s descent. *Curiosity* was the biggest rover to ever land on Mars. *Curiosity*'s landing system was the most complex in the history of space exploration. The team waited nervously to see if it would work.

It took ten years to design and build *Curiosity*. It was part of the Mars Science Laboratory mission. *Curiosity* is equipped with 17 cameras and a mechanical arm for drilling. Its mission is to look for evidence that small life-forms called **microbes** could ever have lived on Mars.

Curiosity was not the first rover to land on Mars. It was the fourth. The rover *Sojourner* had landed successfully in 1997.

◄ ***Curiosity* can take pictures of its surroundings on Mars. It can also take pictures of itself.**

▲ **An artist created an image of what the sky crane system looked like when it lowered *Curiosity* to the surface of Mars.**

Sojourner's spacecraft had landed using airbags. The airbags made the landing bumpy but safe. Two later rovers, *Spirit* and *Opportunity*, landed the same way. But *Curiosity* was five times heavier than earlier rovers. It weighed 2,000 pounds (900 kg) on Earth. It was too heavy for airbags to work. NASA created the sky crane landing system so *Curiosity* could land safely.

When *Curiosity* reached the top of Mars's atmosphere, its spacecraft was traveling at 13,000 miles per hour (20,900 kmh).

As it entered the atmosphere, it heated up to 3,800 degrees Fahrenheit (2,100°C). A heat shield protected the spacecraft. Next, a parachute spread out like a sail. The parachute slowed the spacecraft to about 200 miles per hour (322 kmh). Then the parachute and spacecraft detached from the rover. All that was left was the folded-up rover and the sky crane attached to it.

As *Curiosity* approached Mars's surface, rockets on the sky crane fired downward. They slowed the rover's fall to 1.5 miles per hour (2.4 kmh). Once the rover was 60 feet (18 m) above Mars's surface, the sky crane slowly lowered *Curiosity* down on strong cables. When the rover's six wheels touched the red dirt of Mars, the sky crane detached.

Signals from *Curiosity* were sent back to Earth. "Touchdown confirmed. We're safe on Mars!" announced a scientist at JPL. The team cheered. Scientists hugged one another. *Curiosity* had landed and was ready to share its findings.

Curiosity has provided important information about Mars. More than a decade after landing, the rover is still working. Its landing also proved that the sky crane worked. NASA could now develop bigger and more advanced rovers, knowing that they could land safely. The *Perseverance* rover landed on Mars in 2021 using the sky crane. *Perseverance* continues the important research that *Curiosity* started.

CHAPTER FIVE

REUSABLE ROCKETS

The Falcon 9 rocket lifted off on December 21, 2015. It flew into space from a NASA launch pad in Florida. The rocket was carrying satellites for the company Orbcomm. At first, the launch looked like any other. But the Falcon 9 was about to do something new.

The Falcon 9 rocket was designed by the company SpaceX. SpaceX was founded in 2002 by Elon Musk. Musk wanted to build rockets that could be reused. This had never been done before.

The Falcon 9 is a two-stage rocket. That means there are two sections of the rocket. The first stage is larger. Its nine engines push the rocket off the ground and through the lower atmosphere. After it runs out of fuel, the first stage falls away.

◄ **Landing legs drop down when the first stage of a Falcon 9 lands. The first stage can be reused later for another flight.**

The second stage has one engine. This engine gives the rocket its final push into orbit.

With most rockets, the empty first stage falls back to Earth and crashes in the ocean. A new first stage must be built for each launch. SpaceX wanted to safely land the first stage instead. It could be used for another launch. This could make space flight much cheaper. But landing a first stage is extremely hard. Many of SpaceX's first test rockets crashed when they tried to land. Still, scientists and engineers at the company did not give up.

Three minutes into the December 2015 flight, the first stage fell away. The second stage continued into space. Instead of simply falling, the first stage flipped around and fired its engines. Its computers guided it back to a landing zone near the launchpad. Fins on the rocket steered it through the atmosphere. The center engine slowed the rocket as it fell vertically. Once the rocket was close to its target, landing legs fanned out. The rocket landed gently on the ground. The Falcon 9 had just become the first rocket to carry a satellite into orbit and then land safely back on Earth.

SpaceX successfully landed first stages many times in the following years. Several of them made more than ten trips to space and back. SpaceX's Dragon spacecraft is also reusable.

SPACEX'S FALCON 9 ROCKET

The Falcon 9 rocket is a two-stage rocket. The first stage of the rocket can be reused for later flights after it lands back on Earth.

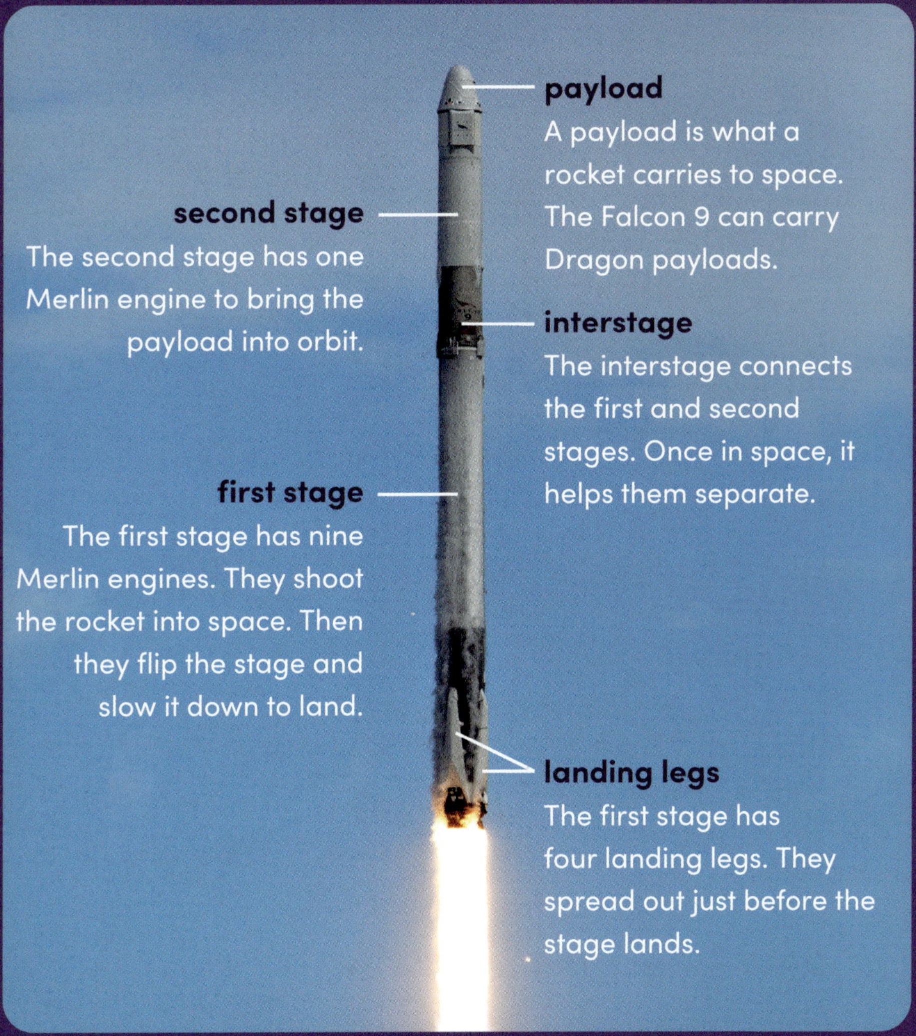

▲ **When a Dragon returns to Earth, it lands in the ocean. Astronauts exit the spacecraft. It can then be reused for another mission.**

Dragon payloads have brought astronauts to the International Space Station. SpaceX is also working on spacecraft to send humans to the Moon and to Mars.

Each milestone in space technology has brought people one step closer to understanding the universe beyond Earth. Spacecraft such as *Sputnik 1* and *Curiosity* have provided scientists with valuable scientific data. The Hubble Space Telescope and the James Webb Space Telescope have seen deeper into space than ever before. The Falcon 9 has made space exploration more affordable and accessible. Technologies of the future will allow humans to explore even farther into space.

THINK ABOUT IT

- Why is it important to explore the universe? What can humans learn from space, and how can this knowledge help improve Earth?
- What are the benefits of having rovers visit planets instead of sending humans? What can rovers do in space that people cannot?
- What piece of technology do you think has changed space exploration the most? Explain your answer.
- If you got the chance to go to space, would you? Why or why not?

GLOSSARY

artificial (ar-tuh-FISH-ul): Something artificial has been made by humans, not by nature. *Sputnik 1* was the first artificial satellite launched into space.

astronomy (uh-STRAW-nuh-mee): Astronomy is the study of stars, planets, and other objects in space. Astronauts need to know a lot about astronomy.

atmosphere (AT-mus-feer): The atmosphere is a layer of gases that surrounds a planet or star. The Hubble Space Telescope orbits above Earth's atmosphere.

microbes (MY-krohbz): Microbes are extremely small living things that can be seen only with a microscope. The *Curiosity* rover was sent to look for evidence of microbes on Mars.

nuclear warhead (NEW-klee-uhr WAR-hed): A nuclear warhead is a type of bomb that produces a gigantic explosion. The R-7 was designed to carry a nuclear warhead.

orbit (OR-biht): To orbit means to travel in a circle around a planet or moon. *Sputnik 1* was in orbit around Earth.

pressurized (PREH-shur-ized): Pressurized means that something is made to stay at the right pressure. Space suits are pressurized so astronauts feel like they are in Earth's atmosphere.

rover (ROH-vur): A rover is a vehicle that is sent to another planet or moon to explore and gather information. *Curiosity* is a Mars rover.

satellite (SAT-uh-lyt): A satellite is an object orbiting a planet. The Moon is Earth's natural satellite.

SELECTED BIBLIOGRAPHY

Manning, Rob, and William L. Simon. *Mars Rover Curiosity.* Washington, DC: Smithsonian Books, 2014.

Neufeld, Michael J. *Milestones of Space.* Minneapolis, MN: Zenith Press, 2014.

Sullivan, Kathryn D. *Handprints on Hubble: An Astronaut's Story of Invention.* Cambridge, MA: The MIT Press, 2019.

FIND OUT MORE

BOOKS

Betts, Bruce. *Space Exploration for Kids.* New York, NY: Callisto Media, 2020.

Downs, Mike. *Invention of Space Exploration.* Vero Beach, FL: Rourke Educational Media, 2020.

Ringstad, Arnold. *Space Missions.* Parker, CO: The Child's World, 2021.

WEBSITES

Visit our website for links about space technology:
childsworld.com/links

Note to Parents, Caregivers, Teachers, and Librarians: We routinely verify our Web links to make sure they are safe and active sites. So encourage your readers to check them out!

INDEX